IN HOSPITAL

KATABASIS

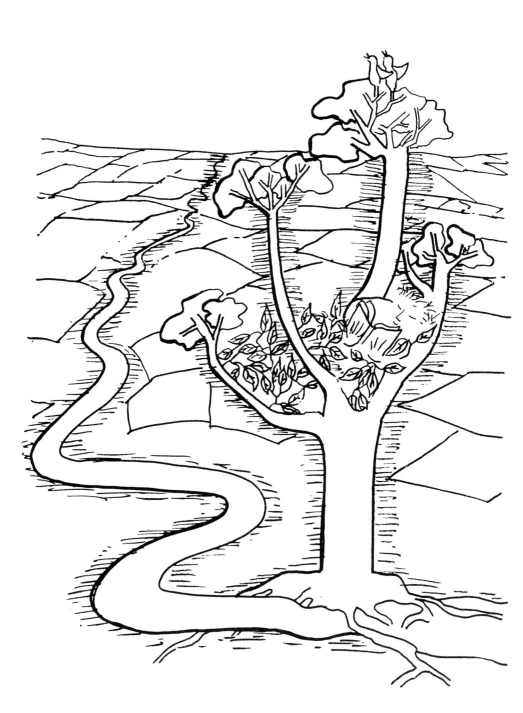

IN HOSPITAL

Two Poem Sequences
100 Years Apart

by
Cicely Herbert
and
W.E. Henley

This book is dedicated
to all who work
for the National Health Service

Copyright Cicely Herbert 1992
First published 1992 by KATABASIS
10 St Martins Close, London NW1 0HR
Typeset by Boldface (071 253 2014)
Printed by SRP (0296 29271)
Cover design by Ella Herbert
The frontispiece is from a Get Well card sent to the author by Elissa Dell.

ISBN 0 904872 19 X
British Library Cataloguing-in-Publication Data.
A catalogue record for this book is available from the British Library.

CONTENTS

Introduction   1

Part 1   3

In Hospital by Cicely Herbert
A Twentieth Century Poem Sequence

Enter Patient   5
Interior   6
Husband, Farewell   7
Music at Night   8
Husband, Good Morrow   9
Before   10
After   11
Nurses   12
Where Do the Dead Go?   14
Physio   15
Highlights of the Day   17
And Here is the News   18
Civilian Victim   19
Hospital Gowns   20
Rose   21
Endymion   22
Tourists   23
Killing with Kindness   24
Words of Consolation   25
No Smoking is Allowed on the Wards   26
Sister is Leaving   27
External Fixator and Surgeon   29
An Object Lesson   30
In December   32
At Midnight   33
Discharged   34

Part 2   37

In Hospital by W.E. Henley
A Nineteenth Century Poem Sequence

Enter Patient   39
Waiting   40
Interior   41
Before   42
Operation   43
After   44
Vigil   45
Staff-Nurse: Old Style   47
Lady Probationer   48
Staff-Nurse: New Style   49
Clinical   50
Etching   52
Casualty   53
Ave, Caesar!   54
'The Chief'   55
House-Surgeon   56
Interlude   57
Children   58
Scrubber   59
Visitor   60
Romance   61
Pastoral   62
Music   64
Suicide   66
Apparition   67
Anterotics   68
Nocturn   69
Discharged   70

INTRODUCTION

I wrote my version of *In Hospital* almost exactly a hundred years after W.E.Henley published his. The two pieces are linked by a coincidence that seems to me too strange to be ignored.

On October 8th 1987 I was brought to University College Hospital after a car crashed with a taxi, lost control, mounted the pavement and ran into me. I thought I'd died but my healthy screams must have convinced passers-by otherwise. My left leg was almost severed above the ankle and I was told an amputation would be necessary. However, in the course of four lengthy operations, the surgeons joined up most of the relevant parts and with substantial bone grafting I now have a functional leg. On good days I walk miles.

After the accident I was given strong doses of morphine and had some entertaining visions. These took place at the foot of my bed where the flowers became a jungle peopled (as I now realise) by characters from life and fiction, who had lost a leg. Among those I recognised were Vuk Karadžić, compiler of the first Serbian dictionary, whose work had recently been exhibited at the British Library, and Sarah Bernhardt. Long John Silver, a childhood favourite of mine, emerged from behind a waterfall and seemed to be trying to reach me.

Some weeks later I was given a copy of Henley's *In Hospital*. As I read it I was struck by the truth of his observation and by how little hospital life and human behaviour have changed since his time. The sequence of twenty eight poems, containing several sonnets and some powerful free verse, has a realism rare in Victorian poetry.

In 1988 I began to research the poet's life and discovered that during the twenty months he spent in the Old Edinburgh Infirmary Henley had become a close friend of Robert Louis Steven-

1

son, author of *Treasure Island*. (It is Stevenson whom Henley describes in the poem 'Apparition'.) Stevenson based the character of the one-legged Long John Silver on Henley. This convinced me that it was Henley himself who visited me in my drug-induced dreams. I decided to write a sequence of poems based on his.

One more link in the story: Joseph Lister, the 'Chief' in Henley's poem, brilliant surgeon and pioneer of antiseptic operations, started his career at University College Hospital. He later spent seven years at the Edinburgh Infirmary, where he successfully treated Henley, who had suffered a tubercular illness at the age of twelve and had already lost one foot. There is a plaque dedicated to Lister in UCH.

During the three months I spent in hospital a series of violent events occurred in the world outside. The eve of my second operation was the night of the Big Storm. Hundreds of trees lay upended like fallen giants in the parks and streets of London. A few days later the Stock Market crash was reported by the press in terms of the death of a terminally sick patient. Next came the tragedy of Enniskillen and then, only ten days later, we heard the warning wail of dozens of ambulance sirens as the injured were carried to our hospital from Kings Cross where they had been trapped underground by fire. Wards were cleared for the casualties but many were dead on arrival. The primitive terror awakened in me by this disaster lay beyond words. A friend repeated like an incantation:

People who have died can't feel pain any more
and the people in pain can be helped.

Cicely Herbert
December 1992

2

PART 1

IN HOSPITAL

Cicely Herbert

University College Hospital, London
October 8th–December 24th 1987

ENTER PATIENT

There were plans for the day
that did not include revisiting
my children's birthplace.

A runaway car
gored me like a bull
tossed me in the air.

My deliverers were two young men
hardly older than my own son;
I needed to know their names.

Bill showed Mark how to make a splint;
he said 'nice and easy' as he gave me
the mask. I sensed that Mark felt queasy.

In the ambulance I recited *Kubla Khan*
(thinking my life depended on it)
but never got beyond the first line.

It was only 9.30 in the morning.

INTERIOR

Alice is alive and living in dizzyland
Alice is alive

In Xanadu an angry wasp
conducts a one-legged band

Alice looks on
where is she

Her flowers are in distress
costly florist sprays buckle in heat
pretty posies melt and neat
bouquets transmute to strange shapes
stale air steams
as beds convert to rafts
and drift past
Chinese lanterns strung
on fragile stalks
tigers undulate under sheets
pale butterflies
writhe on syringes

Alice is alive
I am alive

HUSBAND, FAREWELL

You tug my bedding tight till weight
prevents all movement, like sand
that buries children on a beach.
Your hands deliver a final pat
spades to smooth out cracks.

Outside the covers, my distant leg
is king of a pillowed castle
but I am marooned in this cold mound.
Waves lap me as you vanish
swept off by trafficked night.

MUSIC AT NIGHT

'And chide the cripple tardy-gaited night
who, like a foul and ugly witch, doth limp
so tediously away.'   HENRY V

Night is full of cries and whispers
old women shed years and sob for mother.
Night is not composed of stars
but pain from a dozen wounds.

We heave, we groan, mouth prayers and mantras
and fulminate at grievances that rankle.
We freeze, we sweat, we shake or shout,
bring weary footsteps hurrying to our sides
and swallow pride with pills and water.

Cool hands are solace. A young
exhausted face looks down
moon-glimmer on wychwood.
'If you can't sleep, why not play music?'

Put on the headphones
release the switch. The pilot takes off.
Let the ward and its wailing women
shrink to nothing.

Inside my head, walls and ceiling
are fretted with turbulence
sound dynamites a well-shaft

adagio drops a rope of chords
depth-charged to reach despair.

8

HUSBAND, GOOD MORROW

My morning greeting brims with urgency.
You bend at the knees, the way you're taught
when lifting weights 'to save the back'
and set forth, holding it with outstretched arms.
You cross the polished wood floor carefully
and round the corner to the sluice room
man on important mission.

BEFORE

Like Rapunzel
I'm locked in a turret
insulated from fear.

Do I imagine this banshee
wind wailing?
Pre-med and drowsy
I trace its path as towers upturn
tall chimneys tumble.

Nothing
can touch me now.

I trust the men in white coats
who call to take me away.
Who are they, these messengers
from a Cocteau film?

We're going up and up and up
the place they take me to is
white and hot. Hooded figures
lurk at the edges.
I can't see their faces.

The man who greets me says 'Good morning'
I say 'Laku Noc' to him
Lacu Noc Lacu Noc Laku Noc noc noc noc
nocnocnocnocnocnonononono . . .

AFTER

She is an infant at a cruel birth
who can't remember the dark womb's comfort.
Her bones have been ransacked,
her veins fettered, her skin clamped.
How she needs the needlepoint
to spread numb fire.

Only when they fetch water
she is a lily that unfurls.
Her hands spread in a blue plastic bowl,
they are sponges in a warm sea.
Eyes unstick like shellfish in slow steam.
Shutters in her head release the light
as she floats back into her room.

NURSES

In the tendrils of their care
I leaf and learn again.

Life's better for knowing them
they're fun, down to earth, so young.
I may be mother, but now
I'm utterly dependent.

They wash me, change me, talk to me,
wipe away the spills and tears
clean pin-sites, understand
but do not pander to my pain.

Every morning they pile up pillows
to lift me higher,
an arm under each elbow
and one around my waist, until

a new patient, more ill than me
under investigation
grabs their attention.
At once they are strangers.

Like cattle at dusk their faces
loom in the half-light, voices low
as they struggle with tubes and pumps
to save a life.

I'm left alone
– abandoned –
riding the rocking horse of jealousy
unable to understand anything

as violence envelops
and threatens to topple.

WHERE DO THE DEAD GO?

In hospital
they stop us seeing.

They draw the curtains
when they wheel the dead away.

What is it that they know
too terrible to share?

Where do the dead go?

What if you didn't survive?
What if you're not alive?
Those severed arteries, blood, bone
on the road, were yours.

If death was the bull
who charged, his foot
jammed on the accelerator, then
he left you smashed, tossed
to the pavement

and hell becomes the root
that clamps you to the spot
the grip at your throat
when you can't move,
and you're stuck in a groove
watching it happen
over and over

where the dead go
over and over

PHYSIO

Over and over
the physiotherapist recites
a litany of bones:

'Calcaneus, talus, navicular,
medial cuneiform, sesamoid,
lateral cuneiform, sacrum,
femur, hip, patella,
tib and fib, metatarsal,
calcaneus, talus, navicular . . . '

Metatella tibble fibble petarsel
dopey from drugs we don't retain the names.

She wills us to smile, draws cartoons
of movements we must make.
Her comic heroine's Zazel
a human cannonball with scarlet lips
whose flexi-limbs contort
more readily than ours.

Unmonkey-like, in cots, we cling to the trapeze
no body builders, test our strength with weights
pump muscles, clench our fists, bend knees.
Patient, she applauds each small advance
and promises reward for work well done.
I crave an entertainment 'and it must be good'.

Next day, a junior physio, evening student
at the City Lit of circus skills,
bows to my feet and juggles, just for me.
From such pleasures healing comes.
I crow for joy and swear I will recover.

HIGHLIGHTS OF
THE DAY

cup of tea – breakfast
wash-time
cup of tea – papers
lunch
cup of tea – visitors
cup of tea – tea
cup of tea – supper
medicine
bedtime
cup of tea – lights down

'Nurse
I can't sleep
I'm thirsty
will you make me a . . . '

AND HERE IS THE NEWS

'After a week of fever, the market
has crashed and is in trauma.
Its pulse continues to fall
there's no sign of rally.'

Those who flourished
in the fatter years
fear loss and weep
uncontrollably.

'Stay calm,' is the advice
'and pray for recovery.'

There is panic in the City.

CIVILIAN VICTIM

Another day.
Somewhere out there
a bomb
a nurse's death.

Over the radio
simple as plainsong
the voice of her father
articulates grief.

HOSPITAL GOWNS

Striped blue and white
stained and blotched with blood
that fades to grey, their frayed
and knotted tags don't tie
their sleeves swallow hands.
These short, matted cotton gowns
wrap all kinds of shapes
and each time they're laundered
they're dealt out randomly
making a link.

I think
of all the people before me
who've worn these gowns.
There's a kind of comfort in what we share
(how we're in this together)
comfort from stubborn tallies
that are handed on
in this stumbling human relay race
that has no finishing post
no first prize nor last place.

ROSE

She lies quite still
skin waxy pale
a shaven-headed sarcophagus
who stares at the ceiling.

Sometimes she cries out
shouts angry disconnected words
that seem to curse her mother.
No adult visits her.

At two o'clock most days
her friends pile in
to fidget, lost, at her bedside
in Doc Martens and torn jeans.

They paste her walls with photos
of a holiday they took
– a group of five or six –
last June in Greece.

A close-up shows her springing
from the sea, hands held high
as if in greeting to the sun
cascading curls and brilliant smile

each drop of water on her neck and shoulders
caught by the camera
separate, shining, a perfect whole
held an instant before it fell.

ENDYMION

My favourite cleaner's from the Philippines
and cheerful too, a bonus before rounds.
Her mop seeks spots where dirt's not yet been seen
in calm, broad sweeps that soothe with swishing sounds.
One day, she pauses by my bed to read
some lines by Keats I've pinned up on my wall;
devouring tasty print with gleeful greed
she mouths them silently as if in thrall.
Romantic pragmatist, she likes half-light,
the damp uncertainties of English spring;
now, held by language, alien words excite
and relished sounds spell patterns on her tongue.
'I'll never forget that line,' she tells me, 'never:
"A thing of beauty is a joy forever."'

TOURISTS

They fall from taxis dislocating hips,
trip over paving stones in Oxford Street,
crack elbows at the theatre climbing steps,
break legs in lifts, smash ankles, damage feet.
Cheerful, alert and brave, the blue-haired grannies
phone up their transatlantic distant kin;
they order Fortnum hampers, TVs, trannies,
all week we watch their dearest friends jet in.
We picture hospitals in Hollywood
hygienic, mega-modern private suites
and wonder what they make of stodgy food
and cut-backs, dingy lighting, threadbare sheets.
But when they praise the NHS in loud
approving voices, suddenly we're proud.

KILLING WITH KINDNESS

A shrunken man in tartan dressing gown
calls on the ward each morning after eight
to tempt his wife with sweetmeats from a spoon.
He is a doting and a tender mate.
She's here because he is and she can't last
without his care. His face is grey from cancer.
For twenty years she's loafed in bed; she's vast,
it takes a hoist and winch to pot and turn her.
There's mystery in her lack of will to move;
he's nursed her well, no bed sores on her bum
but she won't smile or say a word. Her love
for him, if it exists, is pretty rum.
What trauma fell to fling her to such hell
remains their secret and they do not tell.

WORDS OF CONSOLATION

What a stupid thing
to go and do to yourself.
I'm telling you, you're on your own.
Not a friend in the world.
You're a bloody nuisance Viv
always have been.

Don't think you're here on holiday.
I've fed the cat
and if there's anything you want
– fags, knickers and that –
I'll get them for you
but you'll have to pay
it's not coming from my pocket Viv
no way.

I've only come to see you're all right
you silly old bugger.

NO SMOKING IS ALLOWED ON THE WARDS

*Patients who want a cigarette can ask to
be wheeled in their beds to the corridor*

A one-armed motor cyclist
is trapped in helpless rage
his naked body squirms in bed
like a weasel's in a cage.

He burns all day in the corridor
an explosive, angry smoker
whose left arm's mutilated
by a tattooed swastika.

SISTER IS LEAVING

After a lifetime
a steady heartbeat may start to flap
like a flock of rooks stuck in a chimney
a car may plough through a bus queue
a millpond become a whirlpool
mountains erupt.

The possibility of chaos
exists everywhere, even
in these good people who nurse us
for whom death itself, is
usually
a sensible affair.

At Sister's leaving party
she is a sacrificial calf
roped and tethered to a wheeled commode
trundled past rows of patients who lie
propped in beds like coconut shies.

She is shoved in the washroom
dunked in the bath
her skin stained a lurid red.

Friends have turned traitor
to hold her under.

She is drowning.

Did she weep then?
Who knows?
When they dragged her out
she might have been a corpse.

But I remember
when she attended to us later
damp hair disguised in neat pony tail
and took our temperatures for the last time
how her hands trembled.

EXTERNAL FIXATOR AND SURGEON

'Fain would I kiss my Julia's dainty leg
which is as smooth and hair-less as an egge.'

                                    HERRICK

He whisks the covers away
a well-trained waiter
displaying Nouvelle Cuisine.
Strong black hairs
have sprouted in the dark.

Gently swinging on its trapeze
this grotesque limb, multiply skewered
splintered bone and cobbled flesh
announces to the world
a feat of engineering.

But faced with my hot human tears
he backs off, out of his depth
like a scolded cat who presents
to his angry mistress
a wounded bird.

Not until spring next year when
shiny skin blooms, healed bones
bear weight, muscles grow strong
and veins regenerate
will I believe, for the first time
in the surgeon's stupendous skill

and my body be mine again.

AN OBJECT LESSON

I'm to be an exhibit
in the lecture theatre today
important consultants are gathered there
to hear what the others say.

I have to display my mended leg
held rigid with metal rods
to a roomful of medical men
bone-setters and orthopods.

> *So wheel me, porter, wheel me*
> *in my supermarket trolley*
> *out of this humdrum ward.*

It's ages before they can see me
they're studying X-rays and charts
and I must sit in the subway
before my performance starts.

Now the doors are opened
they're beckoning me inside
when I'm facing rows of men in suits
I'm shy and there's nowhere to hide.

> *Oh, wheel me, porter, wheel me*
> *in my supermarket trolley*
> *far from their expert eyes.*

My handsome doctor's become quite distant
he's pointing at me with a stick
when he asks for relevant questions
there's a silence and I feel sick.

Then someone says something in Latin
and asks if I can move it.
He regrets that I can't yet retract my foot
and I can't, though I try to disprove it.

Oh, wheel me, porter, wheel me
in my supermarket trolley
to the warmth of Ward 2/2.

When the demonstration is over
and I can go back to bed
I feel that I've failed an important exam.
Was there something I should have said?

IN DECEMBER

On the ward we choose christmassy tunes
for hospital radio requests.
Rudolph the Red-nosed Reindeer,
I Saw Mommy Kissing Santa Claus.
My suggestion *In the Bleak Midwinter*
has been ignored. Any hankering after
the slightly obscure must remain unsatisfied.
Elizabeth wants *While Shepherds Watched*
with Johnny Mathis.
She gets Bing singing *Jingle Bells.*

So when Del picks *The Twelve Days of Christmas*
she doesn't bargain for the operatic version.
Sutherland starts fast and accelerates,
tears through it like a fire engine.
We singalong but Joan's articulation
leaves us miles behind.
In the final sprint our tongues trip up
at 'ten lords a-leaping',
we collapse in disarray.
Dame Joan has won by several lengths.

AT MIDNIGHT

Like tidy gardeners
who dead-head flowers as they fade
porters trundle away the body of Rose
who was asleep in the next bed.

DISCHARGED

Tomorrow
I shall reach the stone highway
down the great curved staircase that connects
the inner to the outside world.
No need now to bump down,
I can get there
using a leg, a crutch, a bannister
perhaps a borrowed arm.

By the front door
clumps of winter chrysanths
wait to be brought in
wilting in cellophane.

In Gower Street
acid fumes hit the throat.
Beyond the shock of light and sound
complicated strands of traffic
stream by, thread all one way
yet somehow navigate
the threatened chaos.

Next year
when I return to look you up
you won't be there.
There'll be other nurses in your place
and other patients too
images of those I knew
like the wrong set of photos
sent back from the printers
familiar shapes and actions matching
unknown names and voices.

At midday tomorrow
you'll call a cab and help me in.
I'll shout out my destination,
turn to wave
and then be gone.

That's how it should be
how it has to be.
In hospital, in time,
we all move on.

PART 2

IN HOSPITAL

W.E. Henley

The Old Infirmary, Edinburgh
1873–75

ENTER PATIENT

The morning mists still haunt the stony street;
The northern summer air is shrill and cold;
And lo, the Hospital, grey, quiet, old,
Where Life and Death like friendly chafferers meet.
Thro' the loud spaciousness and draughty gloom
A small, strange child – so agèd yet so young! –
Her little arm besplinted and beslung,
Precedes me gravely to the waiting-room.
I limp behind, my confidence all gone.
The grey-haired soldier-porter waves me on,
And on I crawl, and still my spirits fail;
A tragic meanness seems so to environ
These corridors and stairs of stone and iron,
Cold, naked, clean – half-workhouse and half-jail.

WAITING

A square, squat room (a cellar on promotion),
    Drab to the soul, drab to the very daylight;
    Plasters astray in unnatural-looking tinware;
    Scissors and lint and apothecary's jars.

Here, on a bench a skeleton would writhe from,
    Angry and sore, I wait to be admitted:
    Wait till my heart is lead upon my stomach,
    While at their ease two dressers do their chores.

One has a probe – it feels to me a crowbar.
    A small boy sniffs and shudders after bluestone.
    A poor old tramp explains his poor old ulcers.
    Life is (I think) a blunder and a shame.

INTERIOR

The gaunt brown walls
Look infinite in their decent meanness.
There is nothing of home in the noisy kettle,
The fulsome fire.

The atmosphere
Suggests the trail of a ghostly druggist.
Dressings and lint on the long, lean table –
Whom are they for?

The patients yawn,
Or lie as in training for shroud and coffin.
A nurse in the corridor scolds and wrangles.
It's grim and strange.

Far footfalls clank.
The bad burn waits with his head unbandaged.
My neighbour chokes in the clutch of chloral . . .
O, a gruesome world!

BEFORE

Behold me waiting – waiting for the knife.
A little while, and at a leap I storm
The thick, sweet mystery of chloroform.
The drunken dark, the little death-in-life.
The gods are good to me: I have no wife,
No innocent child, to think of as I near
The fateful minute; nothing all-too dear
Unmans me for my bout of passive strife.
Yet am I tremulous and a trifle sick,
And, face to face with chance, I shrink a little:
My hopes are strong, my will is something weak.
Here comes the basket? Thank you. I am ready.
But, gentlemen my porters, life is brittle:
You carry Caesar and his fortunes – steady!

OPERATION

You are carried in a basket,
　　Like a carcase from the shambles,
　　To the theatre, a cockpit
　　Where they stretch you on a table.

Then they bid you close your eyelids,
　　And they mask you with a napkin,
　　And the anaesthetic reaches
　　Hot and subtle through your being.

And you gasp and reel and shudder
　　In a rushing, swaying rapture,
　　While the voices at your elbow
　　Fade – receding – fainter – farther.

Lights about you shower and tumble,
　　And your blood seem crystallising –
　　Edged and vibrant, yet within you
　　Racked and hurried back and forward.

Then the lights grow fast and furious,
　　And you hear a noise of waters,
　　And you wrestle, blind and dizzy,
　　In an agony of effort,

Till a sudden lull accepts you,
　　And you sound an utter darkness . . .
　　And awaken . . . with a struggle . . .
　　On a hushed, attentive audience.

43

AFTER

Like as a flamelet blanketed in smoke,
So through the anaesthetic shows my life;
So flashes and so fades my thought, at strife
With the strong stupor that I heave and choke
And sicken at, it is so foully sweet.
Faces look strange from space – and disappear.
Far voices, sudden loud, offend my ear –
And hush as sudden. Then my senses fleet:
All were a blank, save for this dull, new pain
That grinds my leg and foot; and brokenly
Time and the place glimpse on to me again;
And, unsurprised, out of uncertainty,
I wake – relapsing – somewhat faint and fain,
To an immense, complacent dreamery.

VIGIL

Lived on one's back,
In the long hours of repose
Life is a practical nightmare –
Hideous asleep or awake.

Shoulders and loins
Ache . . . !
Ache, and the mattress,
Run into boulders and hummocks,
Glows like a kiln, while the bedclothes –
Tumbling, importunate, daft –
Ramble and roll, and the gas,
Screwed to its lowermost,
An inevitable atom of light,
Haunts, and a stertorous sleeper
Snores me to hate and despair.

All the old time
Surges malignant before me;
Old voices, old kisses, old songs
Blossom derisive about me;
While the new days
Pass me in endless procession:
A pageant of shadows
Silently, leeringly wending
On . . . and still on . . . still on!

Far in the stillness a cat
Languishes loudly. A cinder
Falls, and the shadows
Lurch to the leap of the flame. The next man to me
Turns with a moan; and the snorer,
The drug like a rope at his throat,
Gasps, gurgles, snorts himself free, as the night-nur
Noiseless and strange,
Her bull's eye half-lanterned in apron,
(Whispering me, 'Are ye no sleepin' yet?')
Passes, list-slippered and peering,
Round . . . and is gone.

Sleep comes at last –
Sleep full of dreams and misgivings –
Broken with brutal and sordid
Voices and sounds
That impose on me, ere I can wake to it,
The unnatural, intolerable day.

STAFF-NURSE: OLD STYLE

The greater masters of the commonplace,
Rembrandt and good Sir Walter – only these
Could paint her all to you: experienced ease
And antique liveliness and ponderous grace;
The sweet old roses of her sunken face;
The depth and malice of her sly, grey eyes;
The broad Scots tongue that flatters, scolds, defies;
The thick Scots wit that fells you like a mace.
These thirty years has she been nursing here,
Some of them under Syme, her hero still.
Much is she worth, and even more is made of her.
Patients and students hold her very dear.
The doctors love her, tease her, use her skill.
They say 'The Chief' himself is half-afraid of her.

LADY-PROBATIONER

Some three, or five, or seven and thirty years;
A Roman nose; a dimpling double-chin;
Dark eyes and shy that, ignorant of sin,
Are yet acquainted, it would seem, with tears;
A comely shape; a slim, high-coloured hand,
Graced rather oddly, with a signet ring;
A bashful air, becoming everything;
A well-bred silence always at command.
Her plain print gown, prim cap, and bright steel chain
Look out of place on her, and I remain
Absorbed in her, as in a pleasant mystery.
Quick, skilful, quiet, soft in speech and touch . . .
'Do you like nursing?' 'Yes, Sir, very much.'
Somehow, I rather think she has a history.

STAFF-NURSE: NEW STYLE

Blue-eyed and bright of face but waning fast
Into the sere of virginal decay,
I view her as she enters, day by day,
As a sweet sunset almost overpast.
Kindly and calm, patrician to the last,
Superbly falls her gown of sober grey,
And on her chignon's elegant array
The plainest cap is somehow touched with caste.
She talks Beethoven; frowns disapprobation
At Balzac's name, sighs it at poor George Sand's;
Knows that she has exceedingly pretty hands;
Speaks Latin with a right accentuation;
And gives at need (as one who understands)
Draught, counsel, diagnosis, exhortation.

CLINICAL

Hist? . . .
Through the corridor's echoes
Louder and nearer
Comes a great shuffling of feet.
Quick, every one of you,
Straighten your quilts, and be decent!
Here's the Professor.

In he comes first
With the bright look we know,
From the broad, white brows the kind eyes
Soothing yet nerving you. Here at his elbow,
White-capped, white-aproned, the Nurse,
Towel on arm and her inkstand
Fretful with quills.
Here in the ruck, anyhow,
Surging along,
Louts, duffers, exquisites, students, and prigs –
Whiskers and foreheads, scarf-pins and spectacles –
Hustles the Class! And they ring themselves
Round the first bed, where the Chief
(His dressers and clerks at attention),
Bends in inspection already.

So shows the ring
Seen from behind round a conjuror
Doing his pitch in the street.
High shoulders, low shoulders, broad shoulders, narrow ones,
Round, square and angular, serry and shove;
While from within a voice,
Gravely and weightily fluent,

Sounds; and then ceases; and suddenly
(Look at the stress of the shoulders!)
Out of a quiver of silence,
Over the hiss of the spray,
Comes a low cry, and the sound
Of breath quick intaken through teeth
Clenched in resolve. And the Master
Breaks from the crowd, and goes,
Wiping his hands,
To the next bed, with his pupils
Flocking and whispering behind him.

Now one can see.
Case Number One
Sits (rather pale) with his bedclothes
Stripped up, and showing his foot
(Alas for God's Image!)
Swaddled in wet, white lint
Brilliantly hideous with red.

ETCHING

Two and thirty is the ploughman.
He's a man of gallant inches,
And his hair is close and curly,
    And his beard;
But his face is wan and sunken,
And his eyes are large and brilliant,
And his shoulder-blades are sharp,
    And his knees.

He is weak of wits, religious,
Full of sentiment and yearning,
Gentle, faded – with a cough
    And a snore.
When his wife (who was a widow,
And is many years his elder)
Fails to write, and that is always,
    He desponds.

Let his melancholy wander,
And he'll tell you pretty stories
Of the women that have wooed him
    Long ago;
Or he'll sing of bonnie lasses
Keeping sheep among the heather,
With a crackling, hackling click
    In his voice.

CASUALTY

As with varnish red and glistening
   Dripped his hair; his feet looked rigid;
   Raised, he settled stiffly sideways:
   You could see his hurts were spinal.

He had fallen from an engine,
   And been dragged along the metals.
   It was hopeless, and they knew it;
   So they covered him, and left him.

As he lay, by fits half sentient,
   Inarticulately moaning,
   With his stockinged soles protruded
   Stark and awkward from the blankets,

To his bed there came a woman,
   Stood and looked and sighed a little,
   And departed without speaking,
   As himself a few hours after.

I was told it was his sweetheart.
   They were on the eve of marriage.
   She was quiet as a statue,
   But her lip was grey and writhen.

AVE, CAESAR!

From the winter's grey despair,
From the summer's golden languor,
Death, the lover of Life,
Frees us for ever.

Inevitable, silent, unseen,
Everywhere always.
Shadow by night and as light in the day,
Signs she at last to her chosen;
And, as she waves them forth,
Sorrow and Joy
Lay by their looks and their voices,
Set down their hopes, and are made
One in the dim Forever.

Into the winter's grey delight,
Into the summer's golden dream,
Holy and high and impartial,
Death, the mother of Life,
Mingles all men for ever.

'THE CHIEF'

His brow spreads large and placid, and his eye
Is deep and bright, with steady looks that still.
Soft lines of tranquil thought his face fulfil –
His face at once benign and proud and shy.
If envy scout, if ignorance deny,
His faultless patience, his unyielding will,
Beautiful gentleness and splendid skill,
Innumerable gratitudes reply.
His wise, rare smile is sweet with certainties,
And seems in all his patients to compel
Such love and faith as failure cannot quell.
We hold him for another Herakles,
Battling with custom, prejudice, disease,
As once the son of Zeus with Death and Hell.

HOUSE-SURGEON

Exceeding tall, but built so well his height
Half-disappears in flow of chest and limb;
Moustache and whisker trooper-like in trim;
Frank-faced, frank-eyed, frank-hearted; always bright
And always punctual – morning, noon, and night;
Bland as a Jesuit, sober as a hymn;
Humorous, and yet without a touch of whim;
Gentle and amiable, yet full of fight.
His piety, though fresh and true in strain,
Has not yet whitewashed up his common mood
To the dead blank of his particular Schism.
Sweet, unaggressive, tolerant, most humane,
Wild artists like his kindly elderhood,
And cultivate his mild Philistinism.

INTERLUDE

O, the fun, the fun and frolic
    That *The Wind that Shakes the Barley*
    Scatters through a penny-whistle
    Tickled with artistic fingers!

Kate the scrubber (forty summers,
    Stout but sportive) treads a measure,
    Grinning, in herself a ballet,
    Fixed as fate upon her audience.

Stumps are shaking, crutch-supported;
    Splinted fingers tap the rhythm;
    And a head all helmed with plasters
    Wags a measured approbation.

Of their mattress-life oblivious
    All the patients, brisk and cheerful,
    Are encouraging the dancer,
    And applauding the musician.

Dim the gas-lights in the output
    Of so many ardent smokers,
    Full of shadow lurch the corners,
    And the doctor peeps and passes.

There are, maybe, some suspicions
    Of an alcoholic presence . . .
    'Tak' a sup of this, my wumman!' . . .
    New Year comes but once a twelvemonth.

CHILDREN

Here in this dim, dull, double-bedded room,
I play the father to a brace of boys,
Ailing but apt for every sort of noise,
Bedfast but brilliant yet with health and bloom.
Roden, the Irishman, is 'sieven past,'
Blue-eyed, snub-nosed, chubby, and fair of face.
Willie's but six, and seems to like the place,
A cheerful little collier to the last.
They eat, and laugh, and sing, and fight, all day;
All night they sleep like dormice. See them play
At Operations: – Roden, the Professor,
Saws, lectures, takes the artery up, and ties;
Willie, self-chloroformed, with half-shut eyes,
Holding the limb and moaning – Case and Dresser.

SCRUBBER

She's tall and gaunt, and in her hard, sad face
With flashes of the old fun's animation
There lowers the fixed and peevish resignation
Bred of a past where troubles came apace.
She tells me that her husband, ere he died,
Saw seven of their children pass away,
And never knew the little lass at play
Out on the green, in whom he's deified.
Her kin dispersed, her friends forgot and gone,
All simple faith her honest Irish mind,
Scolding her spoiled young saint, she labours on:
Telling her dreams, taking her patients' part,
Trailing her coat sometimes: and you shall find
No rougher, quainter speech, nor kinder heart.

VISITOR

Her little face is like a walnut shell
With wrinkling lines; her soft, white hair adorns
Her withered brows in quaint, straight curls, like horns;
And all about her clings an old, sweet smell.
Prim is her gown and quakerlike her shawl.
Well might her bonnets have been born on her.
Can you conceive a Fairy Godmother
The subject of a strong religious call?
In snow or shine, from bed to bed she runs,
All twinkling smiles and texts and pious tales,
Her mittened hands, that ever give or pray,
Bearing a sheaf of tracts, a bag of buns:
A wee old maid that sweeps the Bridegroom's way,
Strong in a cheerful trust that never fails.

ROMANCE

'Talk of pluck!' pursued the Sailor,
    Set at euchre on his elbow,
    'I was on the wharf at Charleston,
    Just ashore from off the runner.

It was grey and dirty weather,
    And I heard a drum go rolling,
    Rub-a-dubbing in the distance,
    Awful dour-like and defiant.

In and out among the cotton,
    Mud, and chains, and stores, and anchors,
    Tramped a squad of battered scarecrows –
    Poor old Dixie's bottom dollar!

Some had shoes, but all had rifles,
    Them that wasn't bald was beardless,
    And the drum was rolling *Dixie*,
    And they stepped to it like men, sir!

Rags and tatters, belts and bayonets,
    On they swung, the drum a-rolling,
    Mum and sour. It looked like fighting,
    And they meant it too, by thunder!'

PASTORAL

It's the Spring.
Earth has conceived, and her bosom,
Teeming with summer, is glad.

Vistas of change and adventure,
Thro' the green land
The grey roads go beckoning and winding,
Peopled with wains, and melodious
With harness-bells jangling:
Jangling and twangling rough rhythms
To the slow march of the stately, great horses
Whistled and shouted along.

White fleets of cloud,
Argosies heavy with fruitfulness,
Sail the blue peacefully. Green flame the hedgerows.
Blackbirds are bugling, and white in wet winds
Sway the tall poplars.
Pageants of colour and fragrance,
Pass the sweet meadows, and viewless
Walks the mild spirit of May,
Visibly blessing the world.

O, the brilliance of blossoming orchards!
O, the savour and thrill of the woods,
When their leafage is stirred
By the flight of the Angel of Rain!
Loud lows the steer; in the fallows
Rooks are alert; and the brooks
Gurgle and tinkle and trill. Thro' the gloamings,
Under the rare, shy stars,
Boy and girl wander
Dreaming in darkness and dew.

It's the Spring.
A sprightliness feeble and squalid
Wakes in the ward, and I sicken,
Impotent, winter at heart.

MUSIC

Down the quiet eve,
Thro' my window with the sunset
Pipes to me a distant organ
Foolish ditties;

And, as when you change
Pictures in a magic lantern,
Books, beds, bottles, floor, and ceiling
Fade and vanish,

And I'm well once more . . .
August flares adust and torrid,
But my heart is full of April
Sap and sweetness.

In the quiet eve
I am loitering, longing, dreaming . . .
Dreaming, and a distant organ
Pipes me ditties.

I can see the shop,
I can smell the sprinkled pavement,
Where she serves – her chestnut chignon
Thrills my senses!

O, the sight and scent,
Wistful eve and perfumed pavement!
In the distance pipes an organ . . .
The sensation

Comes to me anew,
And my spirit for a moment
Thro' the music breathes the blessèd
Airs of London.

SUICIDE

Staring corpselike at the ceiling,
  See his harsh, unrazored features,
  Ghastly brown against the pillow,
  And his throat – so strangely bandaged!

Lack of work and lack of victuals,
  A debauch of smuggled whisky,
  And his children in the workhouse
  Made the world so black a riddle

That he plunged for a solution;
  And, although his knife was edgeless,
  He was sinking fast towards one,
  When they came, and found, and saved him.

Stupid now with shame and sorrow,
  In the night I hear him sobbing.
  But sometimes he talks a little.
  He has told me all his troubles.

In his broad face, tanned and bloodless,
  White and wild his eyeballs glisten;
  And his smile, occult and tragic,
  Yet so slavish, makes you shudder!

APPARITION

Thin-legged, thin-chested, slight unspeakably,
Neat-footed and weak-fingered: in his face –
Lean, large-boned, curved of beak, and touched with race,
Bold-lipped, rich-tinted, mutable as the sea,
The brown eyes radiant with vivacity –
There shines a brilliant and romantic grace,
A spirit intense and rare, with trace on trace
Of passion and impudence and energy.
Valiant in velvet, light in ragged luck,
Most vain, most generous, sternly critical,
Buffoon and poet, lover and sensualist:
A deal of Ariel, just a streak of Puck,
Much Antony, of Hamlet most of all,
And something of the Shorter-Catechist.

ANTEROTICS

Laughs the happy April morn
    Thro' my grimy, little window,
    And a shaft of sunshine pushes
    Thro' the shadows in the square.

Dogs are tracing thro' the grass,
    Crows are cawing round the chimneys,
    In and out among the washing
    Goes the West at hide-and-seek.

Loud and cheerful clangs the bell.
    Here the nurses troop to breakfast.
    Handsome, ugly, all are women . . .
    O, the Spring – the Spring – the Spring!

NOCTURN

At the barren heart of midnight,
   When the shadow shuts and opens
   As the loud flames pulse and flutter,
   I can hear a cistern leaking.

Dripping, dropping, in a rhythm,
   Rough, unequal, half-melodious,
   Like the measures aped from nature
   In the infancy of music;

Like the buzzing of an insect,
   Still, irrational, persistent . . .
   I must listen, listen, listen
   In a passion of attention;

Till it taps upon my heartstrings,
   And my very life goes dripping,
   Dropping, dripping, drip-drip-dropping,
   In the drip-drop of the cistern.

DISCHARGED

Carry me out
Into the wind and the sunshine,
Into the beautiful world.

O, the wonder, the spell of the streets!
The stature and strength of the horses,
The rustle and echo of footfalls,
The flat roar and rattle of wheels!
A swift tram floats huge on us . . .
It's a dream?
The smell of the mud in my nostrils
Blows brave – like a breath of the sea!

As of old,
Ambulant, undulant drapery,
Vaguely and strangely provocative,
Flutters and beckons. O, yonder –
Is it? – the gleam of a stocking!
Sudden, a spire
Wedged in the mist! O, the houses,
The long lines of lofty, grey houses,
Cross-hatched with shadow and light!
These are the streets . . .
Each is an avenue leading
Whither I will!

Free . . . !
Dizzy, hysterical, faint,
I sit, and the carriage rolls on with me
Into the wonderful world.